STEPHEN CURRY

The Children's Book

The Boy who NEVER GAVE UP

By Anthony Curcio

SPORTIVA books

www.sportivabooks.com

The Boy Who Never Gave Up: The Stephen Curry Children's Book
ISBN 978-0-578-41172-9 (hardcover)
Text and illustrations copyright © 2016 by Anthony Curcio

ISBN-13: 978-1537010342 (Paperback)
ISBN: 1537010344 (eBook)
Library of Congress Control Number: 2018913331

First Edition

18 17 16 15 14 13   1 2 3 4 5 6 7 8 9 10

BORING STUFF!

NOT BORING STUFF!

Did you know, Stephen Curry was born in the **SAME** state, city, hospital and even hospital floor as fellow NBA superstar LeBron James?!

@ Summa Akron City Hospital (Akron, Ohio)

About the author/illustrator

Anthony Curcio is a five-time best selling author and illustrator on Amazon.com. He has a bachelor's degree in Social Sciences from Washington State University. Anthony is a speaker and television film consultant and producer when not writing books. He lives in Seattle with his wife and two daughters.

Favorite food:	Favorite athlete as a kid:	Favorite sport to play as a kid:
Spaghetti	**Michael Jordan**	**Football**

For more information on Anthony, visit: **www.acurcio.com**

STEPHEN CURRY

The Children's Book

This book is dedicated to my daughters Isabella and Lyla

After dinner one night, a boy sat down to do his homework. He just sat there, staring at the table, daydreaming...

"Mom, do you think I could play in the NBA like dad?"

The boy's mother looked at him with a smile and said, "If you practice enough I think anything is possible, but for now you need to finish your homework."

When the boy finished his homework he went outside and did what he always did. He played basketball.

The boy played other sports too,
but he *loved* basketball.

Basketball was the only sport that really made him dream.

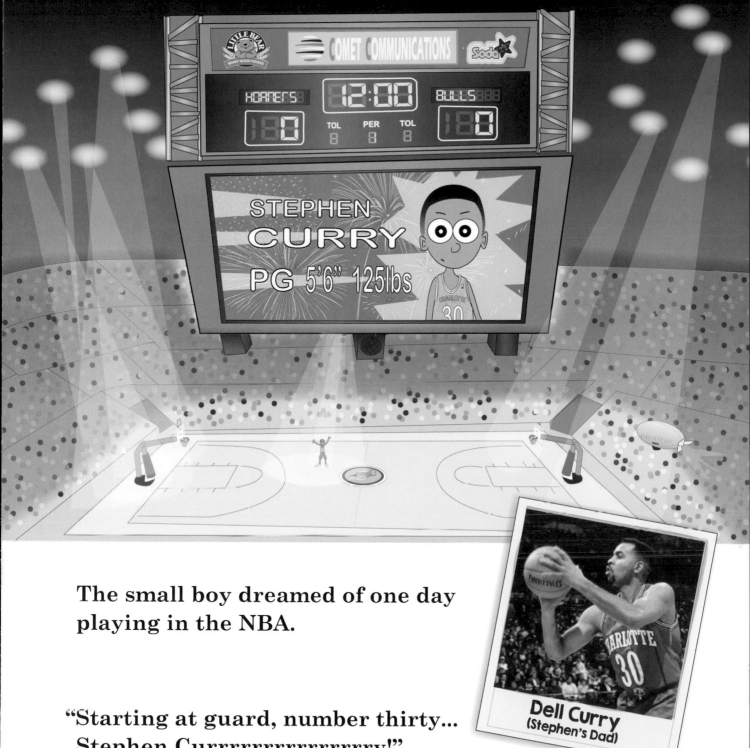

The small boy dreamed of one day playing in the NBA.

"Starting at guard, number thirty... Stephen Currrrrrrrrrrrry!"

"Yaaaaa! Ohhhhhh! Awwwwww!"
Stephen yelled in his best crowd-screaming voice.

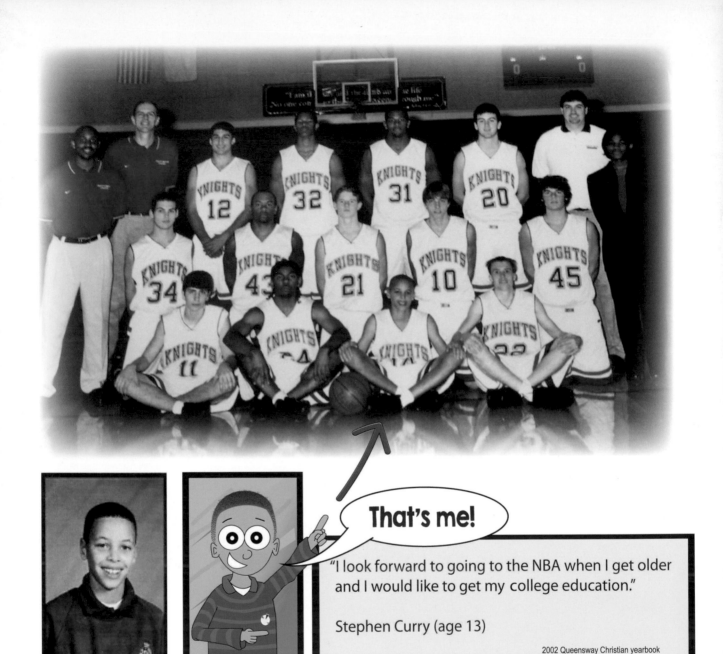

That's me!

"I look forward to going to the NBA when I get older and I would like to get my college education."

Stephen Curry (age 13)

2002 Queensway Christian yearbook

Stephen in 2002 (8th Grade)

The problem was, Stephen was too small and too short. All the kids at school *just knew* that he was too little for the NBA... except for Stephen of course.

"One day, I'm going to play in the NBA just like my dad."

"Hahahahahahaha!" the other kids at school laughed.

"There is *no way* that you'll play in the NBA like your dad."

"He is big and strong and you are small and weak!"

Despite his size, little Stephen kept playing. He became very skilled at dribbling and passing, but because the hoop was so high and he was so short, it was difficult for Stephen to shoot the ball when he was guarded closely.

He was only 5'6" tall and 125lbs as a sophomore in high school. Because he was smaller, Stephen had to work harder and practice more.

One day, Stephen's dad was watching him shoot baskets outside. He noticed how hard Stephen tried to always get better.

"Son, you have more heart and determination than any other player I have seen. I know you are smaller than other players so I want to teach you something that will help."

"The other kids may be taller but if you bring up your shot and learn to shoot faster, they won't be able to stop you."

Stephen did what he always did - he practiced.
It wasn't easy changing the way he shot, but he kept
working every day on what his dad had taught him.
Although, it wasn't work to Stephen because he loved
basketball. When he practiced he still dreamed of
playing in the NBA.

"Starting at guard, number thirty...Stephen Currrrry!"

The following year, all of his hard work showed on the
court. His dad was right, the other players *weren't* able
to stop him.

Stephen led his high school team to three conference titles, earning himself several honors, including being voted one of the best players in the state!

Stephen graduated from high school and was thinking about where he wanted to go to college.

He only wanted to go to one school, Virginia Tech, where his dad had played.

Stephen *knew* he could play there too. All he needed was for them to give him a chance.

Virginia Tech University
800 Washington Street
Blacksburg, VA 24061

Dear Stephen,

Thank you so much for your interest in our school and basketball program.
Unfortunately we are unable to offer you a scholarship.

Best of luck to you,

Stephen Curry
520 W. Main St.
Charlotte, NC 28270

FRAGILE
Game Film

Virginia Tech University
C/O Basketball Program
800 Washington Street
Blacksburg, VA 24061

RETURN TO SENDER

Davidson College
405 North Main St
Davidson, NC 2803

Dear Stephen,

I have watched you play on several occasions and I am impressed.
You are a great player but just as important, you never seem to
give up fighting, regardless of the challenges you are up against.
I would be honored if you would play for me at Davidson College
and have a scholarship for you.

Sincerely,

Coach McKillop

This is Coach Bob

But they didn't. Virginia Tech and many other schools
didn't think Stephen could play on their teams. They
thought he was just too small and not strong enough.
Except for one coach at one very small college.

His name was Bob and he was the coach at Davidson
College. Coach Bob saw what no one else could see.
"Wait until you see Stephen Curry," he told everyone.

Stephen Curry could not be stopped. He led his team to victory over schools that were *ten times* the size of Davidson College, all the way to the Elite Eight.

Coach Bob was right - wait until you see Stephen play!

Stephen broke many records and won several awards. He even led the *entire* country in points scored per game!

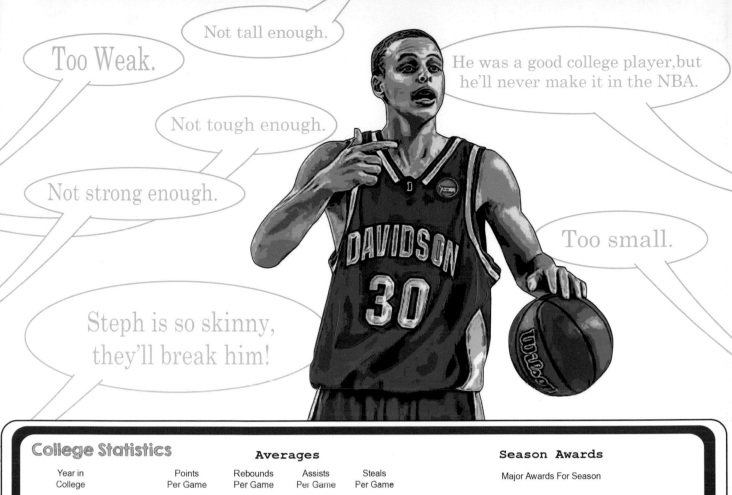

College Statistics	Averages				Season Awards
Year in College	Points Per Game	Rebounds Per Game	Assists Per Game	Steals Per Game	Major Awards For Season
Freshman	21.5	4.6	2.8	1.8	Conference Freshman of the Year
Sophomore	25.9	4.6	2.9	2.1	Second-Team All-American
Senior	28.6	4.4	5.6	2.5	First-Team All-American

People who watched Stephen play in college started to see what Coach Bob had seen all along. Many were beginning to believe what Stephen had always believed about himself.

But there were still many people that said Stephen was just too small to play in the NBA. They said he got lucky, that he wasn't strong enough, that he wasn't good enough. They just kept talking and talking.

But Stephen didn't listen.

He was too busy winning the NBA's Most Valuable Player Award *twice*, leading the league in scoring and steals, taking his team to NBA Championships and pretty much breaking every 3-point record that has ever existed.

Stephen was told he was too short in high school, too weak in college, and not good enough to play in the NBA.

He has proven that never giving up is *more* important than being the biggest, the tallest or even the strongest. But most importantly, Stephen Curry has proven that...

Dreams come true!

COOL CURRY FACTS

After reading **The Boy Who Never Gave Up** you now know where Stephen wanted to play in college, but do you know why?

Virginia Tech University

Steph's dad, Dell played **both** basketball and baseball at Virginia Tech AND his mom, *Sonya* was on the **volleyball team!**

He also wears

 # **30** because it was his dad's number in college and during Dell's **16** year NBA career.

Dell played 10-seasons straight with the Charlotte Hornets.

No player in team history has scored more points while wearing a Hornets jersey.

Steph's favorite player growing up?

MUGGSY BOGUES

Who's that?

Muggsy Bogues was Dell's teammate on two NBA teams and would play games against young Stephen in pre-game warm-ups and practice. Muggsy was a point guard and will forever be known in the NBA. He is the shortest player in league history, standing only **5'3"** tall! **five-feet, three-inches!**

Stephen's brother, Seth also plays in the NBA, most recently with the Portland Trailblazers.

Stephen's sister, Sydel was a four-year letterman in volleyball at Elon University in North Carolina.

While still in elementary school, Stephen already was a star!

Steph and his dad were in a Burger King commercial!

actual photo taken from the 1990's commercial

CURRYSCHOOL

All 3 Curry kids went to the same montessori school.
Their parents, Dell and Sonya founded the school.
Their mom was the principal, grandma the cook.
The school still exists today, but isn't called the Curry School!
Christian Montessori School of Lake Norman

Can you figure out the WarDELLriddle?

Stephen is "Stephen's" middle name, NOT his first name...
Stephen was named after his dad, former NBA player Dell Curry.
His real name is the exact same as his dad's... **but it's <u>not Dell</u>. What is Stephen's first name?**

"Dell" was a nickname that more than just stuck, it pretty much became his name (on basketball cards, in rosters, etc.) Both Dell and Stephen share the exact same name: Wardell Stephen Curry and Wardell Stephen Curry II.

If you liked *The Boy Who Never Gave Up*, be sure to check out,

The Boy Who Became King

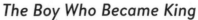

The Boy Who Became King is the inspiring true story of NBA Superstar LeBron James. It tells the story of a young boy and his loving, single mother and their struggle to make it on their own.

With the help of a coach and his family, LeBron is introduced to the game of basketball. Against all odds, "the kid from Akron" not only makes it to the NBA but becomes a basketball legend who now helps others who are struggling like he and his mother once were.

The Boy Who Became King is the inspiring true story of NBA Superstar *LeBron James*.

Color all of your favorite NBA Superstars, compare stats, design team uniforms, shoes and much, much more.

available NOW on AMAZON.com or SPORTIVABOOKS.com